Just for Today

Jesus is Enough

Strength from God's Word

Sharon Hurkens

Avid Readers Publishing Group

Lakewood, California

Sharon Hurkens

15 Donald Place East Rockaway, New York 11518

www.shedawayministries.com

Book Layout ©2014 BookDesignTemplates.com

Just for Today! Sharon Hurkens. —1st ed.

ISBN-13: 978-1-61286-265-1

Printed in the United States of America

Contents

I would like to dedicate
this work to all those who love to apply
God's Word to their everyday situations
and allow Him to direct their paths.

We don't see things as they are,
We see them as we are.
—Anais Min

The more we study God's Word and learn to apply it to our everyday life, the easier it will be for us to leave behind the past or any situation which entangles us and prevents us from walking in the life of fulfillment that we can walk in.

Sharon Hurkens

[1]

The Lion Roars, Should you be Afraid?

"Stay Alert! Watch out for your great enemy, the devil. He prowls around like a roaring lion, looking for someone to devour." 1Peter 5:8

THE LION, OR KING OF THE JUNGLE, is a very intimidating animal. If you had to meet it face to face, you will be afraid. If he suddenly roars your heart might stop. Growing up in South Africa, we were able to get up close to lions in a game reserve. To me there is nothing more magnificent, powerful, yet terrifying. Once, we came so close to a pride of lions, they walked right past the vehicle we were in, that if we reached out, we could have touched them. On this last occasion the lead lioness turned her head and I looked straight into her eyes. Much to my surprise they were stone cold. It wasn't "kitty, kitty," no it caused my heart to drop. "Wow", I thought, "if I was on

1

the ground she would not think twice but to devour me." She would not be able to do otherwise, that is her nature.

Scripture refers to Satan as a "roaring lion." Let's get a character profile on our enemy, Satan. This may help us to be aware of his devices. He is true to character.

Scripture once again gives us the answer on Satan and his tactics.

...He was a murderer from the beginning. He has always hated the truth, because there is no truth in him. When he lies, it is consistent with his character; for he is a liar and the father of lies. John 8:44

When a lion roars, he throws his voice and this causes his/her prey to become confused and terrorized. When the devil tries to bring confusion and fear into your life, don't give in and run. Stand firm in your faith even if your knees are shaking. The same Jesus who indwelt Paul dwells within you.

Peter tells us how to resist the devil.

"Stand firm against him, and be strong in your faith. Remember that

your family of believers all over the world is going through the same kind of suffering you are." 1 Peter 5:9

How do you stand firm? You must know who you are in Christ, not who you are in yourself, but in Christ. Affirm it in prayer and in your lifestyle.

The name for the devil, Satan, is found fifty-four times in the Old and New Testament while "devil" is used thirty-four times and only occurs in the New Testament. The Greek word for devil is *diabolos* which means "an accuser, a slanderer"

The Hebrew word for Satan is exactly that, *Satan* which means adversary. An adversary is someone who accuses, slanders and resists.

We are not fighting a war where we can see our enemy. However, God did not leave us unprotected. He has equipped us with everything we need to overcome and be victorious. We just have to apply what God has given us to our lives. In other words, Stand Firm in your faith. Know who you are in Christ.

****

Prayer: *Lord, I thank you for loving us so much and for equipping us with everything we need to fulfill your plan for our lives while we are on earth. Give me the wisdom and strength to resist Satan instead of accepting his lies as truth. Help me to stand on your word and to quote it every time I feel attacked. I believe You are the truth and I desire to walk in your ways. Open up the doors for me so that I can clearly see which ones are from you. Thank you for coming to give me a life of fulfilment.*

Your Turn:

In what ways do you feel that you are being attacked right now?

[2]

A Horror Story then Love Stepped in

So they arrived at the other side of the lake, in the land of the Gerasenes. When Jesus climbed out of the boat, a man possessed by an evil spirit came out from a cemetery to meet Him. Mark 5:1-2

THE STORY ABOVE continues on to say, that the Lord cast the demons out of the man into the herd of pigs and the pigs rushed down into the lake and were drowned.

Those looking after the pigs could not believe their eyes and went to report what had happened. Everyone came to Jesus then and they saw the man who had previously been possessed sitting there dressed and in his right mind.

This man was a total outcast, no one wanted to have anything to do with him at all, they had tried to bind him with chains but that would not work. Then Jesus came into His life, showed him mercy and he was set free.

You see, Jesus does not judge us in our present condition or state of mind, He sets us free from the chains that hold us and cut into our flesh, He gives us a sound mind. He does not treat us like the rest of society, because His nature is love and compassion and He came to show us how to live and treat each other as well as setting us free.

I pray that you too will want to experience the freedom offered by Christ. Let our Lord free you from whatever is holding you back from receiving His presence which is love incarnate.

What we see from this account and many other accounts in the Bible is that no matter how bleak our situation may seem to us or how hopeless our life might seem, nothing is impossible with Jesus. God sent His Son so that you and I can be free and live life to the fullest. Any other lie that you may believe is contrary to God's Word, even through the toughest trial, you can feel God's presence with you.

****

Prayer: Thank you Jesus that you have died so that we can be set free from our chains that keep us from walking in the amazing plan you have for our lives. Help me to remember that you do not condemn me, but set me free.

Your turn:

What are the chains holding you back from walking in God's amazing plan for your life?

[3]

What is that in your Hand?

Then the LORD asked him, "What is that in your hand?"
"A shepherd's staff," Moses replied.
Exodus 4:2

WHEN GOD ASKED MOSES this question, he was not aware of the potential that God saw in the staff.

So often we don't see the potential in the things that God has given to us. Neither do we know our gifts and abilities He has equipped us with.

Another example is David's life. Just a simple shepherd's rod yet it became the visible symbol of the invisible God.

"He picked up five smooth stones from a stream and put them into his shepherd's bag. Then, armed only with his shepherd's staff and sling, he

***started he started across the valley to
fight the Philistine." 1 Samuel 17:40***

Here we read of how David took his
slingshot with the stones he had picked
up and the next thing, the giant Goliath
was slain. Could David have done it
without God's help? I don't think so, God
was there with David.

Could Moses have parted the Red Sea or
delivered the Israelites from the clutches
of Pharaoh? Never.

These are just a few scriptures where we
can see how God took whatever there
was and worked miracles. God does not
expect us to do things if we do not have
the capacity or ability to do something.
He does not ask more of us than we are
able to do.

What do you have in your Hand? Has God
given you the ability to speak, the ability
to teach, the ability to lead, to share His
love or serve?

We find ourselves in situations where it
seems impossible for God to meet our
needs, never mind help us to react to those
circumstances with faith and integrity.
This is exactly what He promises though.
Let us ask God for His presence and His
strength to overcome our lack of faith.

Let us trust Him to use that which He has placed in our hand to further His kingdom.

When God asks you to do something for His kingdom and you answer "But Lord, I ...." God answers with "What is that in your hand?"

****

Prayer: Jesus, I know that you have a task for me to accomplish while I am here on earth, please take whatever abilities and skills I have to further your Kingdom. Thank you for equipping me for such a task.

Your Turn:

What is it that you have "in your hand?" What can God use to further His Kingdom through you?

[4]

The Art of being Anxious for Nothing

Don't worry about anything; instead, pray about everything. Tell God what you need, and thank Him for all He has done. Then you will experience God's peace, which exceeds anything we can understand. His peace will guard your hearts and minds as you live in Christ Jesus. Philippians 4:6-7

HAVE YOU EVER BEEN TOLD over and over by a well-meaning person such as your spouse, friend or family member that Scripture says we are not to worry, nor be anxious over anything?

This is one of the hardest disciplines to practice or to make a reality in life. There are always things that pop up every day that cause anxiety in our lives. We become anxious over our jobs, over our families, our finances, our future, etc and the list just goes on.   It is a difficult thing to be a Christian, because we know what the Scriptures say yet how do we make them a reality in our lives?

Have you noticed how children go through life? They do not even give a thought to any worries about the future or how they are going to get through next week. They just know that their parents will do their best at providing for them.

God who is our heavenly Father, will also guide us in the best path for us. All we need to do is trust Him and walk faithfully in what He calls us to do.

As adults we tend to either live in the future or the past. Worrying about what tomorrow will bring, or the mistakes we made and live with regrets.

God does not want us to live in the past nor worry about tomorrow and its problems.

We are to *"Rejoice in Today"* and be glad in the day that God has given us.

Are there situations that we need to solve? Of course, but for the most part we are to bring everything to God for He cares for you and your life. Everything about you is precious in His sight. Don't waste your time waiting until everything is perfect before you start enjoying what you have. Your present situation is precious and worrying about the yesterday's or the tomorrows will not change the "now."

Prayer: Jesus your word is so clear regarding our concerns and cares about what we will eat, or wear. Your word tells us to bring everything to you, laying it at your feet and resting in your peace which you give us. I lay my cares and stress at your feet Lord, take them from me and give me your peace which surpasses all understanding.

Your Turn:

What are you worried about?
List them and give them to God. Walk into your days knowing that God heard you.

[5]

A Call to Choose Life

For this commandment I am giving you today is not too difficult for you, and it is not beyond your reach. It is not kept in heaven, so distant that you must ask, 'who will go up to heaven and bring it down so we can hear it and obey?' No, the message is very close at hand; it is on your lips and in your heart so that you can obey it. "Now listen! Today I am giving you a choice between life and death, between prosperity and disaster." Deuteronomy 30:11-15

AS HUMANS, BOTH CHRISTIANS and non- Christians alike, we are basically selfish in nature. We want what we want and we want it now. Oh, and we want God's blessing on our life as well. Time is short and we are all scrambling for more of it to accomplish our work, tasks at home and responsibilities with family, church and any other project that needs to get done.

First on our list though is "God please bless my day, protect me, my family and help me to get through this trial." We pray this as we're driving of course. While driving, the man in front of us slams on his brakes and we almost hit the rear of his car. Suddenly prayer is out of the window, cut short and thoughts or words fly across our minds and out of our mouths.

The car moves off and we continue driving. Maybe we will remember where we were in our prayer or we will just go on thinking about the difficult day ahead of us.

Time out to "Be still and know that I am God?" no, not likely. God must give you the peace and quiet the turmoil in your heart, mind and soul, while you are running through the day.

Today, we have the Holy Spirit to help us to obey what the Lord wants us to do. Jesus did not leave us orphans. God's word says in the above portion that everything that He commands us to do is possible.

Oftentimes, we just shrug our shoulders and think that what God is expecting us to do is too difficult, but really, it is not.

This is one of the most beautiful promises to us; nothing is too hard for us.

I want to encourage you to remember that God's plans for you are always good. It is not to destroy you, but to bless you.

You are not alone in your daily struggles, God is always with you. When you feel like you are sinking, cry out to Him and He will help you. He wants to hear from you. Remember, He cares for you more than anyone else can because He created You!

God wants to invest in your life. He needs your time.

****

Prayer: Jesus thank you that you care so much about ME! Thank you that you give me a choice to choose life. Help me to remember that I must listen to your voice and always make the choice that will give me life.

Your turn:

What do you think is too difficult for you to do right now? What choices do you have to make which you find are impossible to make?

Remember God's plans are not too difficult.

[6]

A Killer Lurks

Herod was furious when he realized that the wise men had outwitted him. He sent soldiers to kill all the boys in and around Bethlehem who were two years old and under, based on the wise men's report of the star's first appearance. Herod's brutal action fulfilled what God had spoken through the prophet Jeremiah: Matthew 2:16-17

JESUS CAME INTO THIS WORLD to give those who believe in Him as their Redeemer a life of purpose and one where they can live in a state of peace which surpasses all understanding despite the world crisis looming. John 10:10a clearly reveals to us that Satan plans to take away any purpose of life and state of peace from anyone who will believe his lies.

Following the star, the Magi came from the East to find Jesus. They were not sure where to find Him so they went to Herod to enquire of him where to find the newborn King.

Ah Ha! Here comes the killer. These innocent men went off to find out exactly where Jesus was born and how to get there. They go to Herod and excitedly tell him of the Savior's birth. Envy enters Herod's mind and Satan's plans to kill Jesus is put into effect.

God's plan of course was that Jesus fulfilled His purpose on earth. Satan thought he could thwart that plan of Salvation.

When you and I accept Christ as our Redeemer, we give our lives to God so that His plans for us will unfold. Satan tries to foil those plans which God has for us. We need to keep our minds and our focus on God's truth, not what Satan puts across our path.

We always stand on the brink of a New Challenge. One filled with promise and hope. Yet, opinions cross our minds such as "you don't matter to God." Or "Before you can be a vessel of God you first have to be a man or woman of the world tasting of everything it has to offer before you can know what it is to be a Christian, one who has been redeemed from a life of sin." These thoughts are there to spoil God's plans for your life. Nowhere in Scripture do we read of an account such as these statements.

My word of encouragement to you is as you stand at the brink of new challenges, you wholeheartedly surrender your life to the Lord. Place your complete trust in His hands. Ask for His guidance before you take any action. Remember, it is He who created you. He formed you in your mother's womb, not so that Satan can delude you, no! So that His purpose can be fulfilled through you.

Prayer: Jesus, I place my life into your hands. I stand at the edge of a new challenge, a new day, go before me and make my path straight. Give me wisdom to discern what is from you and give me the strength to make the right choices.

Your Turn:

What thoughts, actions or challenges thwart God's plans in your life?

[7]

An Image Bearer

Then God said, "Let us make human beings in our image, to be like us. So God created human beings in His own image. In the image of God He created them; male and female He created them. (Genesis 1:26a, 27)

I HAVE ALWAYS HEARD the statement over and over again that we are created in the image of God. We represent Him in every way throughout our lives. When we rub shoulders with people in the subways, in the elevators, the streets, our workplace and family, we are showing what Jesus is like. This often scared me and made me feel guilty because I am by no means perfect as He is.

This is exactly what Satan would like us to experience. He does not want us to believe that God created us uniquely, even though imperfect. As long as we walk

21

around remembering our imperfections and shortcomings, we are unable to cause the effect that God created us to cause.

The Scripture in Genesis about us being created in His image really hit me between the eyes. I always used to struggle with a low self-image. Then for the hundredth time I read through Genesis one day and this portion jumped off the page.

It was then that I started to do research into this whole issue of being "An Image Bearer."

I am a Christian firstly. When I look at myself, not necessarily in the mirror, but at my inner conviction, I not only remember who I am in Christ but I see who I am. This enables me to stand taller, walk by faith each day listening to the still small voice of God's Spirit living and transforming me from the inside out.

It is not "I" who moves mountains, causing people's lives around me to change. It is God Himself. I am just a broken shapeless vessel, in the process of being shaped into the person He wants me to become.

My personality has huge flaws, my human heart can be extremely wicked sometimes.

This is how God is seen through our shortcomings. We are weak, He is the strength. He uses us, yes, the imperfect people we are and brings about His will on this earth.

Slowly, our lives change, because and only because we submit our minds, hearts and souls to His directives.

A Scripture in James emphasizes this so well.

But if you look carefully into the perfect law that sets you free, and if you do what it says and don't forget what you heard, then God will bless you for doing it. James 1:25

Take the challenge of being God's Image Bearer and walk uprightly, letting Him change you and bring about the awesome change in those you touch. We are weak, but He is our strength. When we see God working through our human frailty to bring about the changes in this broken world, we are blessed, encouraged and joyful.

Go! Be that Change someone needs.
Go! Cause the Change that we all need.

Go! Because in the beginning God said "Let us make man in our image, in our likeness..."

I no longer feel guilty about being an Image Bearer, I proudly walk as one, even though I am imperfect. He is seen through my imperfections because He brings about change around me.

Prayer: Jesus, thank you that You are my strength, You are the Change Maker in my own life as well as equipping me to cause change around me in other people's lives. Help me to see myself through Your eyes. Help me to walk and stand tall.

Your Turn:

What is preventing you from seeing yourself as an Image Bearer of God, the Creator of the Universe.

[8]

A Time for Everything

For everything there is a season, a time for every activity under heaven. Ecclesiastes 3:1

I WAS IN THE GARDEN ONE Spring morning with the dogs and the birds were singing, flowers were starting to bud, squirrels were running and chasing one another and the air smelt "fresh," Ahh, a lovely change in season.

It doesn't matter at what stage we are in our lives, whether a sad one or a period of loss and confusion, it will end and a new season is around the corner.

Solomon was a wise man and even though throughout Ecclesiastes we read that he does not really draw a pretty picture of "life" and situations. In fact, he goes on to say that "what is life worth, after all". But in chapter 3, he depicts a beautiful scenario of "life" in a positive manner.

Remember that all things have a season and God wants us to take a deep breath and enjoy the life that He has given to us. It is a discipline that must be worked on, I totally agree. This is something that does not come naturally, but with each day and season (situation), God is teaching us to wait on Him, trust Him in all things and His peace is ours.

This is a concept that people in general do not understand, but as Christians we have this beautiful promise from God.

May you experience the beauty in each season of life, this day.

Prayer: Jesus, that you that you created the different seasons. Thank you that as each one comes around it reminds me of how my difficult challenges in life will come to an end and each day is to be enjoyed for its different facets. Help me this day to take in a deep breath and relax in your care.

Your Turn:

What is preventing you from enjoying this day and season of your life?

[9]

Almost Devoured

...The thief's purpose is to steal and kill and destroy. My purpose is to give them a rich and satisfying life. John 10:10

HALLOWEEN COMES AROUND once a year. Kids and adults shop for their costumes trying to find the scariest outfits in the neighborhood.

Candy specialists have bagged everything so conveniently for treats that you cannot even walk out of the store without one of their well marketed bags of chocolates.

Just as the above picture is smack in the middle of a paragraph and you can't miss it, so too we cannot escape the seasonal graphics around us.

Consideration is not even given to the fact that there is a different aspect to the whole "dark side" or "underworld." This is the perfect and acceptable plan of Satan, the enemy of your soul.

As much as I would love to tell you that there is no-one out there who is trying to steal, kill and destroy your lives and those of your children, I cannot do that. I have experienced firsthand the subtle lie of the enemy and how he tried to steal my youth away as well as my future.

Even under the protection of my Christian parents, Satan managed to get in to my life without a "hitch." It began as a game, enticing me to join in with his sick scheme. He accomplishes this with whomever he can.

Satan knows that God placed within us a curious nature, because mankind was created to explore, bear fruit, multiply, and use their God-given potential and brain to create beautiful effects. He also knows we are equipped with our own potential to choose life or death. Lying is his nature; he schemes, twists and distorts even the truth. He can never be trusted or believed. God on the other hand, cannot lie. He is truth, our source of hope and distributor of life to whomever wants it.

As his scheme to steal away joy, peace, hope and blessing begins to intensify, parents please listen to your children if they experience difficulty sleeping, difficulty in achieving goals as well as being overly anxious for no particular reason. Children are especially targeted as they are innocent and looking for acceptance as well as excitement. Satan will provide them with all that but at the cost of losing their peace which God alone can provide as well as their hope of a future.

Being children of God we have the upper hand over any scheme the devil tries to attempt. We are conquerors and victorious. The few simple actions and words we speak will accomplish God's eternal redemptive plan for us. James 4:7 gives us in a few words, the action we can take if we experience evil around us. He says ... *"Resist the devil and he will flee."*

Adults may know who they are in Christ, but children still need to be protected until they know who they are in Christ.

Christ brings Life and Hope, Satan represents death and hopelessness. Choose Life for your family.

Prayer: Please Lord help us to discern the evil schemes of satan. Give us the strength to walk away from his ways. Instead, give me your peace and direction for my life as well as for the lives of my family members.

29

Your turn:

In what way has Satan managed to deceive you?

Has he stolen your peace? Your hope for a life of fulfillment?

[10]

Experiencing Joy in Opposition

Sanballat was very angry when he learned that we were rebuilding the wall. He flew into a rage and mocked the Jews, saying in front of his friends and the Samarian army officers, 'What does this bunch of poor, feeble Jews think

They are doing? Do they think they can build the wall in a single day by just offering a few sacrifices? Do they actually think they can make something of stones from a rubbish heap – and charred ones at that?"
Nehemiah 4:1-2

HAVE YOU NOTICED that there are circumstances that seem to prevent your faith in Jesus from growing? Well, Satan will do anything to keep you weak and susceptible to attack. As you grow and mature in Christ, the protective wall of faith that guards your heart becomes more and more impermeable to attack. In Scripture we read of Nehemiah who rebuilt the walls of Jerusalem but in the process of rebuilding them he faced a lot of opposition.

Sanballat was the governor of Samaria and the opposition to Judah. If Jerusalem was unprotected and the people are unmotivated, then Sanballat could control them. He did not like strong leaders like Nehemiah who was not afraid to rebuild the wall and motivate the Jewish people. Sanballat was afraid that he would lose his power and influence over the Jewish people.

When people can't control or manipulate you they become angry and try to intimidate those around them; this is precisely what Sanballat tried to do to Nehemiah and his workers so that they would stop their work on the wall.

These people faced opposition because they tried to make positive changes in their lives. They tried to turn their circumstances around for the better. There will always be people in your life who want to keep you "down", whether they are family members, friends, or acquaintances.

We do face opposition in life, yet Scripture declares that we can keep our joy despite the circumstances.

We should have a plan of attack to combat the enemy of our soul who brings discouragement and fear.

We should protect our weak areas and pick up our weapons. What is our weapon? The Word of God is our sword. (Ephesians 4:17) We should use the Scriptures to counteract the negative words or attacks on us, such as the doubt that comes in like a flood washing away the promises of God.

Nehemiah continues to encourage his people with the fact. *"...Don't be afraid of the enemy! Remember the Lord, who is great and glorious, and fight for your brothers, your sons, your daughters, your wives and your homes!" Nehemiah 4:14b*

Each morning, we are to "Put on" God's armor. Pray the words of Scripture and counteract all lies with the truth from God's Word. Pick up your sword and fight! God is your strength and your song.

Prayer: Jesus thank you for being my strength and my song. Thank you for equipping me with all the tools I need to

stand and fight those who try to bring me down. Go with me into this day and help me to stand strong against the enemy of my soul.

Your turn:

What is your weak area where you need to stand strong and fight your enemy?

[11]

A Listening God

For I cried out to Him for help, praising Him as I spoke. If I had not confessed the sin in my heart, the Lord would not have listened. But God did listen! He paid attention to my prayer. Psalm 66:17-19

GOD CAN HEAR everything and his love for us is unconditional but our fellowship with Him is not. It is such a privilege to have a personal relationship with God and we should realize that in any relationship, there has to be communication and this is between both parties being "present and sincere."

God is all knowing and sees everything. He does not only see the "outside appearance" but our inner thoughts and our hearts as well.

We cannot expect to enjoy a relationship with God when our hearts are not sincere.

Have you ever heard yourself praying? We usually have a huge bag of burdens to lay down at the Lord's feet, and because we have a relationship with Him, He bears our burdens every day. Not once has God ever turned me away from His presence, Not once has God ever not taken time out for me. People are not always able to bear our burdens, but God gladly offers to take them from us and give us His peace.

If you are not experiencing the reality of God bearing your burdens, then maybe you should examine how you come to Him with them. Do you "dump them and run?" Do you have the attitude of: "God, why are you not ...?" or "God do...?"

Remember God is not our spouse or child or someone we can order around, He wants to have a relationship with us which means we come respectfully into His presence, thanking Him for everything that He has done for us, praising Him for who He is,

then making our requests known and thanking Him again for hearing our cry.

God waits patiently for you to fellowship with Him! His arms are open. I have never seen a picture with God's arms closed, have you? He is saying "Come! spend some time with me and I will give you rest."

Prayer: Lord, because you are all knowing and ever present in my life, I ask that you remind me that communication is a two way street and I must wait on you as well. Help me Lord not to bring all my cares and concerns only without hearing from you.

Your Turn:

How well do you wait on God for His responses to your cries?

[12]

I Want ...

Elkanah had two wives, Hannah and Peninnah. Peninnah had children, but Hannah did not. 1 Samuel 1:2

WHAT IS IT that I don't have, yet so badly want in my life? How is this reality of not "having" what I so desperately want affecting the way I live my life from day to day?

John Newton said, *"There is many a thing which the world calls disappointment, but there is no such a word in the dictionary of faith. What to others are disappointments are to believers intimations of the way of God"*

The text in 1 Samuel is just one of the many texts in the Bible which I can relate to in a very strong way. "Peninnah had children, but Hannah had none"

I am Hannah. Just like her, I "have none"

Dealing with trying to have children yet not having any has been one of the longest journeys of faith and disappointment all at the same time. Several years of going through the motions of trying to "fit in" the normal family situation was the most trying times in my life. Doctor after doctor and test after test has testified to the fact that there is no reason why my husband and I cannot have what we wanted, which was children, like everybody else had.

Advice came from well-meaning people and cards and notes encouraging us to have "faith", maybe we did not "believe" enough. But I have had to face the hard, cold truth. There is something else that God wanted for my life. He wants me to take this pain and void in my life and use it for His glory.

When dealing with this issue of the hope of a child then losing that hope through a miscarriage over and over again, there are a lot of lessons that I have learnt in life. Dealing with people over and over again I have come to realize that it is not whether or not a person could or could not have children. There will always be issues where we live our lives focusing on what we don't have, and this blinds us to all we do have. There are people who have allowed their inability to have what they think they wanted or needed so badly that it tore families apart. We often do not realize how much we have, and I'm not talking about tangible "stuff" I'm speaking about families that we do have, friends and most important a God who cares about and knows every inch of our pain.

Author Mary Webb penned this well known statement many years ago. ***"The well of Providence is deep. It is the buckets we bring to it, that are small."***

We should take the lessons that we learn from all our disappointments and mo-ments of crisis in life. They create perseverance in us and teach us to "run" to the Master and spend time with Him for our strength.

We should never come to our Father with small buckets. Because Heaven's Providence overflows in such huge ways that even during the times of our lives when it appears we are missing out on what we long for the most, God is going to surprise us with something tremendous and we had better come prepared to receive this massive outpouring for our buckets will be so full. We will have enough not only

for us but there will be plenty spilling over into the lives of everyone we touch.

Prayer: Father God, I come to you today with a void in my heart. This void Lord is because I so desperately want something in my life which I cannot have. Help me Lord to see that if You do not answer my prayer and give me what I am asking for, then its because You have a different plan for my life and I thank you for that.

Your turn:

What is it in your life that you so desperately "want" that it affects your relationship with God?

[13]

Where is Your Faith?

One day Jesus said to his disciples, "Let's cross to the other side of the lake." So they got into a boat and started out. As they sailed across, Jesus settled down for a nap. But soon a fierce storm came down on the lake. The boat was filling with water, and they were in real danger. The disciples went and woke Him up, shouting, "Master, Master, we're going to drown!"

When Jesus woke up, He rebuked the wind and the raging waves. Suddenly the storm stopped and all was calm. Luke 8:22-24

GOD ALLOWS US TO encounter fear-provoking circumstances to teach us how to trust Him in any circumstance. The disciples found themselves in a very dangerous situation. The storm made it impossible for them to sail across the lake. Jesus was tired from the burdens of the day and fell asleep, the boat began to fill with water and it appeared as if they were in danger of sinking at any moment.

Jesus did not only calm the storm on the water, He also calmed the storm inside the hearts of the disciples.

What do we learn from this story? Faith does not prevent the storms of life. Jesus did not hold the disciples responsible for the storm, but he held them responsible for their response to the storm. They had given in to a very human fear: they were afraid they were going to die. The enemy, Satan, can stir up storms around your life. Your faith in God will not prevent these attacks but may actually attract them. When the storms come, you are not to give in to the notion that your faith has failed, but rather that it is being tried.

No storm ever comes up against us without divine permission. The enemy has limitations. But God allows us to confront a fear-provoking circumstance so that we can face them head on, whether it is an economical storm, a vocational storm, a physical storm, or even a marital storm, faith does make a difference in how you deal with the storm.

Fear is a natural thing which ordinary human beings experience, yet we can rest in the person of Christ. We can rest in the promise of Christ. Whatever Christ commands us to do He enables us to do the task, just as He wanted the disciples to go with Him to the other side of the lake, He would enable them to handle any obstacle while crossing over

Faith also rests on the performance of Christ. Look back over your life and see how God has helped you face the obstacles and get through them. We have the Bible which is the complete revelation of His faithfulness and sufficiency. Reading the Bible encourages faith!

The last two thousand years have been filled with testimonies concerning the faithfulness and adequacy of Christ. And we also have our own experiences to prove God's faithfulness.

If you are living by your fears instead of by your faith Jesus asks you "Where is your faith?" With that question He is asking you to cast all your cares on Him for He cares for you.

Prayer: Jesus, please help me to place my complete trust in You. Help me not to fear the unknown or fear what tomorrow may bring. Help me to place my faith and confidence in You and You alone.

Your Turn:

What do you fear?

Where is your faith?

[14]

Beauty for Ashes

"To all who mourn in Israel, He will give a crown of beauty for ashes, a joyous blessing instead of mourning, festive praise instead of despair. Isaiah 61:3

GOD GIVES US surprising promises at times when we feel we have blown it and all is at a loss. When it seems that what we see is that there is no way this piece of the puzzle is working "together for good."

With God there is forgiveness and restoration and a fresh new beginning. Jesus foretold Peter that he was going to deny Him. When Peter did, He did not condemn him, no, instead He took Peter from that failure into a ministry which has reached to every believer in succeeding generations.

We can depend upon God's super-abundant grace to transform our hurts, disappointments, failures, sins – even abuses – into benefits, our buffetings into blessings, and our failures into comforts. God's grace transforms our lives, takes the ashes and makes it into something beautiful and useful for His Kingdom.

Our perspective of God is so narrow. We look for God to come into our lives in circumstances and events that please us. Oswald Chambers says we need to give God elbow room. *"Always be in a state of expectancy and see that you leave room for God to come in as He likes."* Give Him the right to be God in our lives.

If we can only see the bigger picture of our lives, the way God has it planned, we will confidently go into each new day expecting God to be with us and guiding us in all the decisions we have to make.

We should always go about our day with the thought in our mind, "Ok, God sees the situation, He wants to be glorified in this situation, how can I bring glory to God through my decision making in this situation. When all is said and done, no matter what career we are in, the only thing that will matter is what you did for God and His Kingdom. When we realize that we are ambassadors for the creator of the universe, we may just do things a little differently. We will care about one another; and we will care about those who do not know Him in a personal way yet.

Go into this day knowing that God sees your whole situation; He sees the "bigger picture". It is such a comforting thought.

Prayer: Jesus thank you for taking my pain and giving me your comfort, strength and peace during this difficult time. Help me to remember that you know the end result of my life and how this difficult time will end. Let me glorify You despite my circumstances.

Your Turn:

What is your difficult situation right now which is taking away your joy?

[15]

You, God's perfect Design

You watched me as I was being formed in utter seclusion, as I was woven together in the dark of the womb. You saw me before I was born. Every day of my life was recorded in your book. Every moment was laid out before a single day had passed. Psalm 139:15-16

GOD FIRST DESIGNED you in His mind with a final purpose. Then, when the timing was right, He "created" you. With the fine details that He knew you would need such as your personality, your heart, your desires, and the intricate thoughts that He knew you would have.

Before the prophet Jeremiah was born, God had in mind that he would be a prophet and so everything about Jeremiah was made with him being a prophet in mind. God knew that he would need a tough personality. He knew that Jeremiah would love Him and serve Him in that area, all the days of Jeremiah's life.

Before David was born, God "designed" him to be a musician and a great songwriter. He knew that he would be a king one day and so created him with talent and gifts so that he would be able to fulfill the purpose that God wanted for him.

I can go on forever giving you all the descriptions of the various people who are mentioned in the bible, the many Kings, Queens, Judges and warriors, but that would take a whole book.

You and I are no different. I want you to think about the fact that just as God "designed" everyone in the bible, He "designed" you. His plan for you had a final purpose from the very beginning, before you were even thought of by your parents, before you were in the womb.

When you look in the mirror you might not think that God ever had a purpose for you being alive. Well, God never makes a mistake and He never would waste a life when He sent His Son Jesus to die for you. So you are not just a being without a soul. You were created for a purpose and He knows exactly how beautiful that plan is for your life.

Remember Joseph? Well who would ever have imagined that he was going to rule and become such a great man? When his brothers sold him, what do you think went through his mind at the time? *Oh man, I'm dead.* Yet he didn't die, No, God had a plan for His life and it was fulfilled.

May God bless you today and I pray that you will ask God to reveal His beautiful plan for your life, don't waste any more time. Walk in His plan, it's great.

Prayer: Lord Thank you for loving me in such a deep and special manner. Thank you that you created me with a specific and unique purpose in mind. Help me to realize who I am in You. Help me to see myself as you see me.

Your turn:

Who do you think you are? What are your specific talents, gifts and desires that will help God's Kingdom grow?

[16]

EWWW,
What's that smell?

"...Fix your thoughts on what is true, and honorable, and right, and pure, and lovely, and admirable. Think about things that are excellent and worthy of praise." Philippians 4:8

EVER NOTICED how college students usually save up all their laundry for when they come home every few months so that mom can make it smell clean and fresh again?

My brother was in the army in the 70's and my mom and I were so excited to go and pick him up for a month of vacation. His name is Reg and he is the oldest of the five siblings.

Reg came out carrying his belongings in a dilapidated, torn green army bag, threw it in the car and then came to where we were waiting for him under a huge tree.

It was such an exciting moment, but as we were getting closer to the car, Reg said "I'm really sorry mom but my clothing is filthy." My mom was so pleased to be taking him home that she replied: "Oh, that's ok, it can't be that bad." Then we opened the doors of the car and jumped in only to be welcomed by this nauseating odor. Reg was not joking about his clothes being filthy, ugh, they stank.

Neither my mom nor I wanted to be rude, so we just ignored what we knew was disgusting, as if the odor would just go away. Well, we traveled for about 30 minutes and it really wasn't stinking so much anymore. By the time we got home, we could not even smell the filthy clothing. This made me think about what we as Christians do in the workplace, or some of the places we have to spend time in.

Most times, in the workplace, there are people who use foul language, at first it makes us uncomfortable, but later on we adapt and may even use the curse words ourselves. Often times we have a family member who uses God's name in vain. We are most uncomfortable at first, then it doesn't seem to be that bad after a while and we may find that it pops out of our mouth so easily, and no one flinched. Next time, it gets easier and before we know it, we are changed to be like the world, instead of us transforming the world. The result unfortunately is that the message of Hope which we have to deliver does not get out, so those people who needed it go on living without it.

We tend to absorb our surroundings; the negative people color our world, instead of us bringing about the reality of God and His love.

My challenge to everyone is that we should consider our environment. What are you absorbing and in turn giving to others? Many times our environment is something we cannot change, but we are able because we have the Holy Spirit within us, to encourage others and help them to soak up the love of Jesus who will in turn fill their hearts and minds with His peace. We need to model this first ourselves.

Scripture has several portions found in the Song of Solomon discussing the beautiful fragrance of perfume. But Isaiah 3:24 highlights a different odor. *"Instead of a sweet smell there will be a stench;*

Imagine for a moment if we could reflect on the beautiful passage of Philippians 4:8 We will be immersed in the fragrance of God's Word and in turn spill it over to those who need a lift in their spirit.

Prayer: Lord help me not to accept those things in my life which are a stench to your nostrils. Highlight the avenues in my life I need to surrender to you and depend on your strength to change. Help me not to live in my dirt until it is no longer seen as dirt, but as a part of me. Take it from me.

Your Turn:

What are the items in your life which are unclean. Ask God to help you clean your life up, inside and outside.

[17]

Powerball Winnings

"My purpose is to give them a rich and satisfying life." John 10:10

THE TICKET LAY in front of me on the kitchen table, two hundred and forty million dollars. A winner was announced and I was that winner. Two Hundred and forty million dollars gave me a sense of euphoria which was uncontainable. My husband and I sat stunned, looking at the winning ticket.

What now? First of all we will pay off all our bills, then we will buy a home, then we will get furniture for the home. Will we retire? Will we keep working? Oh so much excitement and so many life changing decisions to make. Then... I felt a lick in my face and my little Yorkie Poo woke me up. It was all a dream. I had not won the Powerball, and in fact had not even bought a ticket.

The harsh reality that I had not won a dime yet had experienced the euphoria of winning enough money to give me a life of peace and contentment left me nauseous and sitting straight up in bed wanting to cry.

Forcing myself out of my stupor, I suppressed my desire to sob like a baby. I got out of bed and took the dog outside. The fresh air outside cleared my depressed mind and my heart skipped a beat. Imagine over two hundred and fifty million people clamoring to win the money, literally getting into debt at their futile attempts.

Over two thousand years ago, God sent His Son Jesus to live as a man and die so that you and I can inherit eternal life if we just believe that He is our Redeemer. What bigger winning ticket could we receive? Wow! Even while on earth we can experience life to it's fullest because Jesus came.

Suddenly, my heavy heart was replaced with an inner joy. I am a winner of one of the biggest gifts ever known to man. And I want everyone to enjoy the same winning ticket with me.

John 3:16 says *"For God so loved the world that He gave His only Son, so that everyone who believes in Him will not perish but have eternal life.* God did not send His Son into the world to condemn it, but to save it." We need to believe in our Redeemer and live life with purpose and Hope. May this be the day you live that life of abundance realizing who Jesus is. He is our Hope, He is God with us. He is our Provider, our Healer, our Protector and so much more. Who needs powerball when we have such a winning offer?

The gift of Life Eternal.

Prayer: Thank you God for sending us Jesus so that we can live forever with you. Thank you that we have the winning ticket by believing your Word.

Your Turn:

What is preventing you from realizing that you have the biggest gift ever?

You are a WINNER!

[18]

Roots

Let your roots grow down into him, and let your lives be built on him. Then your faith will grow strong in the truth you were taught, and you will overflow with thankfulness. Colossians 2:7

HURRICANE SANDY TOOK its toll on many trees when it hit land. Some trees held their ground for several hours of the battering wind, but others gave in shortly after Sandy hit and crashed to the ground crushing cars, roofs, and power lines as they succumbed to the power of the storm.

Many people lost their entire possessions and homes. Memories were washed away as the water came in to their homes and took whatever was in its path. This was certainly a devastating experience for anyone to have incurred.

When the storm had passed and the debris had settled, I walked through the neighborhood and saw these beautiful enormous trees toppled as if they were twigs. What I noticed was their roots were not very big. This is mainly one of the reasons they could not stand their ground. The water softened the ground and when the wind blew, they succumbed to their fate of death.

Immediately I thought of our lives as Christians and how applicable the shallow roots were to our relationships in Christ. How deeply are we rooted and grounded in our faith as Christians. Do our roots reach deep into His word or do we merely hear the Scriptures and sermons, yet never applying it to our situations.

The Colossians had not merely received the doctrines of Christ, they had received Christ Himself. Notice, the verb "received" which means more than the moment a person asks Christ into his or her heart. Paul used the word to describe the transmission and safeguarding of traditions and teachings from one person to another. They were reminded of when they received Christ Jesus and their new status as members of Christ's body.

Having Christ dwell in us through His Holy Spirit, we should walk and conduct our lives in union with the indwelling Christ. The verb indicates a continuous action: "continue to live."

Paul used the metaphors in these verses, first telling believers to walk, then to be rooted like a plant, built like a building and established like a legal document.

Being rooted in Christ is the same as a tree or plant would draw nourishment from the soil through their roots, so the believers should draw life-giving strength from Christ. The more we draw strength from Christ, the less we would be fooled by those who falsely claim to have life's answers. Our faith in God would not waiver and we would see His Hand on our circumstances even during times of storm.

This storm has brought to light whether we are rooted in Christ or rooted in a superficial idea of Christianity. I know for myself, this storm made me realize that it is not possessions so much that God cares about but He certainly cares about "life." Many people did die in this storm but considering the millions affected by it, I can see that God protected our lives.

This period of unrest has also taught me to surrender that which I have no control over. I could not protect or even encourage those who needed it in the beginning of the storm because there was no contact with anyone.

What life lessons did any of your storms teach you? I hope that it was to appreciate the breath in your lungs, each beat of your heart and that each day brings the promise of God's miracles all around us. Take time to look at God's imprint on your lives as well as those around you.

Prayer: Lord thank you for the breath in our lungs. Thank you for the precious gift of life. Help me to realize that my spiritual roots must be embedded in you.

Your Turn:

What do you place value in in your life? How deep are your spiritual roots?

[19]

The Sun is Always Shining.

"Don't worry about anything; instead, pray about everything. Tell God what you need, and thank Him for all He has done. Then you will experience God's peace, which exceeds anything we can understand. His peace will guard your hearts and minds as you live in Christ Jesus."

Philippians 4:6-7

I RECENTLY FLEW to Denver to attend a writer's conference. On the flight from JFK to Detroit I sat next to a Jewish girl. At first she did not respond when I greeted her nor did she even glance my way for most of the wait before takeoff. The weather was miserable and the clouds were thick and dark. This caused the ascent to be very bumpy, but after about twenty minutes the plane's nose broke through the thick layer of clouds and there was nothing but beautiful clear sky with the sun shining brightly.

This triggered an excited response from the young lady. "See that?" she blurted out to me with the biggest smile on her face.

"Yes, it's beautiful, isn't it?" I responded trying to generate the same excitement she had. I was thinking to myself "okay, I don't know what is so exciting but glad you are happy."

"The sun is always shining." She began to inform me. "Even if the clouds are thick and dark, it's still sunny above them. It's just like life. You can be experiencing the worst day possible, but soon the bad experience you are having passes. We just have to remember that the sun is still shining even though all we can see is the thick dark clouds."

I must admit, her excitement rubbed off on me and I could clearly see her point of view. Whatever situation you are facing right now, it may be a dark gloomy one where you cannot see a positive outcome. But, remember who you are in Christ and that He will never leave nor forsake you. All you have to do is approach His throne confidently, laying all your petitions at His feet and He will give you the peace that surpasses all understanding.

The clouds may threaten and thunder may sound, but soon, the sun will shine again. It may be a while, but the sun will show itself again and it is always shining above your situation.

Prayer: Lord thank you that you know everything about my present situation. Thank you that even though I feel as if the sun will never shine again, it will. You will help me through this situation and the darkness will lift.

Your turn:

What is the situation you are facing right now which seems to make you feel as if you are living under a perpetual cloud?

[20]

The Day which Rocked the World

So they took Jesus away. Carrying the cross by Himself, He went to the place called Place of the Skull (in Hebrew, Golgotha). There they nailed Him to the cross. John 19:17-18

ASK ANYONE WHICH day they think changed the world and you will get all sorts of answers. An older person might say December 27, 1941, when Japan bombed Pearl Harbor. I often said that September 11, 2001 changed our world.

But really? The day which changed our world forever was when Jesus went to the cross for our sins. There were no news reporters, no lights and no cameras. Tom Brokaw didn't flash on the screen. President Obama was not even born yet. There were no shockwaves reverberating around the world as they do whenever something devastating happens. But, when Jesus rode on the back of the donkey and entered into town at the beginning of the week before His crucifixion, the world was changed.

Yet many people still do not believe in the death and resurrection of Jesus and put it all down to tales told down through the ages.

The unchanging message of the church is the gospel. The church is founded on it. It is not thriving because of someone's personality, a social cause or even a need. The church exists because of the gospel.

The message of the church is that Christ died and has been raised from the dead.

Lives are changed because of the truth of the Resurrection of Jesus Christ. People have Hope.

The Resurrection of Jesus Christ is the Hope of the world. This week is an excellent opportunity for you to rock someone's world with the Gospel. Christ, in You, will help you reach the lost.

I challenge You! Go on and Rock the World.

Prayer: Thank you God for Rocking our World by sending your only Son Jesus to die on a cross for us, so that we can have life eternal with you.

Your Turn:

When would you say your World was Rocked?

[21]

The Plans of a Mother

"For I know the plans I have for you," says the Lord. "They are plans for good and not for disaster, to give you a future and a hope." Jeremiah 29:11

WE HAVE WITNESSED one of the biggest weddings on the planet in all its splendor and fanfare, the wedding of a prince, namely Prince William and, Kate Middleton. Never in Kate's wildest dreams did she ever think that she was going to be a woman with so much purpose and influence. She is now a princess.

I watched a few of the scenes which were played during the day and particularly loved the scene where her father walked her down the aisle. What was he thinking? If someone would have told him when Kate was born that she was going to rule and be Queen of England down the road, he would have laughed and said, "ok, dream on."

As mother's hold their newborns in their arms, they dream of what great purpose she/he is going to have. Parents always plan a path for their children and hope they will accomplish far more than they have ever accomplished. I know my mom had her plans for me. I was to stay close, get married, have kids, and never iron a shirt, or wash windows, or dust. Never in her wildest dreams did she think that I was going to live on another continent in one of the largest cities in the world with my own dreams and desires, far different from what she would ever have thought or wanted for me.

My nephew's wife just gave birth to a handsome little boy and as I looked at his picture, I found myself planning a path for him and he is not even my son. Imagine what his mother is planning.

Scripture has so many amazing examples of mothers and their sacrifices for their children. One of the biggest sacrifices of course was Mary, mother of Jesus. Another great example was Jochebed, mother of Moses.

We all know how the life story of Moses turned out, what an amazing young man of influence and purpose.

He made his mistakes, but God had a plan for his life and when He knew Moses was ready to walk in that plan, He revealed Himself to Moses. There are far too many people of purpose to mention, but all their mothers at one time held them in their arms and had plans for them. God on the other hand knew why He created them and why He brought them into this beautiful world.

Another beautiful example is that of Esther, she had no father or mother but an uncle who raised her. Imagine that for a moment. Surely there were times when Esther thought she would never amount to anything or anyone of purpose. God knew He had her life in His hands. She saved the Jewish nation from extinction, another child of purpose.

My challenge to you parents is that as you look at your children, first ask God's direction and call on their lives, then do your best to guide your children to first look to God before they make any decisions in life. This will save them a lot of stress later on in life it will give them more time to work for God in whatever capacity it is He purposed for them.

I know from experience that if only I had taken God up on His challenge sooner, I would have had less struggles in my life's decisions and career choices. There is nothing that I haven't tried, only to find that I had no peace inside. I tried to "work for God in the choice of careers which I chose, only to find, I quit soon afterwards.

I have surrendered to Him and His plan for my life, I have never been so content and excited about what lies ahead. God's ways are good, His plan for our lives is perfect.

Prayer: Thank you Jesus for the great plan you have for my life. Help me to ask You which direction to take so that your plan for my life can be fulfilled.

Your turn:

What plans do you have for your life? What plans do you have for your children or family members? Have you first asked God what His plans are?

[22]

Wounds caused by a Bite, a Look, or a Roar

You will trample down lions and cobras;
you will crush fierce lions and serpents
under your feet! Psalm 91:13

GROWING UP IN a beautiful land such as South Africa had its benefits, yet there were always dangers lurking, as there are in any country. I grew up on a small holding which was home to many dangerous snakes. Almost every day, my mom was killing a snake. They would slip in through a gap in the door to find protection from the elements outside. I would meet these slithery creatures either by surprising them when I opened up a cupboard to get something out and there would be this huge snake taking a nap and not happy at all to be disturbed.

Mothers are not afraid of much when it comes to protecting their children. Even though my mom was afraid of snakes, she knew that she had to kill them immediately before they escaped and brought family members with them the next time they came in. After slamming the cupboard door shut, I would run screaming to find my mom. "Snake, snake." Or when I was younger, "Nake, nake." My mom would then take a shovel or an axe and go to take care of the evil lurking in my room. I clearly remember my mom saying on her way to the room "Oh dear Jesus, help me to kill this snake and protect us from their poison." I would be right behind her, "Yes, Jesus, protect us. Go kill him ma..."

Sometimes, the snake got away before she could kill it, and other times, found it close to where it was first seen. I do not miss those days at all and nor does my mom. Each time my mom would smack the snake with the shovel she would say.. "you pest, you dog, you evil, die..." now, looking back, it is hysterical. Then it was not so funny. Not once however, did she ever use a bad word. Now as an adult looking back, I can honestly say, if I was killing a snake? I don't know if I would not use a bad word or two.

What can our feet do to protect us against such terrible monsters? Nothing. These are spiritual wickedness's. Each of these animals causes wounds in various ways. All these animals are dreaded by anyone who happens to meet them on their way. They cause us to fear and tremble, yet with God on our side, we can stand up to them.

Even though we do not encounter many wild animals in our day, there are other temptations, fears and situations we face which bring about the same intimidation as do the snake, lion and cub. Whatever the enemy is or whoever he/she is we face daily, Christ has given us the authority to overcome without succumbing to their threat.

The psalmist tells us that if we go in God's way, trusting Him to uphold us, then we will "tread on the lion and the cobra" we will "trample the great lion and the serpent." In Christ the righteous will be victorious over Satan too.

Sometimes I think it would be easier, if it were an animal we were facing, rather than the silent causes of fear, temptation, lies and threats of Satan. The stronger our relationship with God though, gives us the inner strength to rise up against our enemy. We resist the fear, the lies, the threat of death and he flees.

What is it causing you to run screaming "Snake, snake, lion, dragon...?" Get to know who you are in Christ and the snake, lion or dragon will no longer be so intimidating. Will they forever disappear? No. But you will be able to face them easier each time and resist whatever it is they are trying to do to you or cause you to do. Never run in fear or hide, lift your head, hold it high, face any snake in confidence. You have been given the authority to stamp on them.

Prayer: Thank you God that you have given us power and authority over the evil one. Help me to remember who I am in You and defeat my enemies.

Your turn:

What are you afraid of or Who are you afraid of? In light of God helping you defeat those who are against you, how does this fact help you?

[23]

You can kill the Giants in your Life:

"For I can do everything through Christ, who gives me strength." Philippians 4:13

WE ARE ALL familiar with the account in Scripture of David and Goliath. Goliath was a Giant who terrorized God's people.

As he was talking with them, Goliath, the Philistine champion from Gath, came out from the Philistine ranks. Then David heard him shout his usual taunt to the army of Israel. As soon as the Israelite army saw him, they began to run away in fright." 1 Samuel 17:23-24

Often, those we rely on to give us encouragement during difficult situations or wisdom, we are given advise such as "Oh think positively and things will change.

77

Well, in this situation there is no room here for positive thinking. No, what's needed is positive Action. When Goliath said, **"Come here, I want to throw your flesh to the birds of the sky",** we see that there is a distinct difference here in David just thinking positively and acting positively.

See the difference between just thinking about killing our giants and actually acting on it?

In our opening Scripture verse, Paul makes that great statement in Philippians. Here we see that there are distinct points to help us in this verse make the positive changes. I c*an,* is positive thinking. I *can do* is the positive action. I *can do all things* is the positive faith. Paul then says how we can do these by saying; **I can do all things through Christ.** That is positive power.

When we face the "Giants" in our lives, remember that we do not attack them by how we see ourselves or our ability but we see God in us.

Whatever it is that you face, or whatever changes you need to make, You Can with the Power of the Lord in you. That Power is His very presence, the Holy Spirit.

The Giants in your life can be destroyed.

God gives us the power and strength that we can make the things which seem too large and overpowering in our lives, go away.

Prayer: Lord, You are my source of strength. Please help me to overcome any obstacles in my life which seem to be preventing me from moving ahead in the beautiful plan which you have for my life. Help me to see my Giants through your eyes.

Your turn:

What are the Giants in your life preventing you from achieving what God has planned for you?

[24]

Even in the belly of a fish

"I cried out to the Lord in my great trouble, and He answered me. I called to you from the land of the dead, and Lord, You heard me!: Jonah 2:2

HAVE YOU EVER wondered if there were times and places where God would not be able to hear you crying out to Him in your distress?

This week I was reading Jonah and what really ministered to me was that Jonah prayed to God from inside the fish. He said:

If ever there were a place where I would think that God would not hear your cry would be from the stomach of a huge fish. This is such a source of encouragement to me because it does not matter where we are in the world, or how dark our situation seems, God is able to hear us when we cry out to Him.

Jonah goes on to praise God for bringing him up from the pit. He experienced first-hand what it was like to feel his life ebbing away, but Jonah remembered God and began to cry out to Him.

Jonah continued to praise God for whom He is and God delivered him on dry ground. Often times we expect our deliverance to be quick, easy and clean, but it doesn't always work out that way. The cleaning up of our lives may take some time, effort and a whole lot of patience, but with God's hand working out our plan we experience salvation and are set free from bondage.

When God asks us to do something for Him, there are times when we try to justify our decision not to be obedient. If He wants to particularly work through us in a specific situation, then He will continue to lay it on our hearts, opening and closing doors until we are obedient and follow His plan.

Just as Jonah delayed going to Nineveh, we too delay in doing what we should for God. God is so merciful though and when we find ourselves stuck in a pit which seems dark and circumstances are unpleasant, God waits patiently for us to cry out to Him, praising Him even though we are still in the pit of despair, He then takes us out, helping us to clean up and move ahead so that we can be a part of His Great Plan.

Are you experiencing God drawing you to do something for Him? I want to encourage you not to delay. Don't get yourself into such a bind before you answer the call from God. Be blessed and enjoy what He has for you to do. It is awesome!

Prayer: Thank you Jesus that I can call out to you no matter where I am or what I am doing. You hear my cry. Give me the strength to obey you.

Your Turn:

Where do you think it is impossible to reach out to God.

[25]

Grace, Sweet Grace

Then Jesus said: "Come to me, all of you who are weary and carry heavy burdens, and I will give you rest."
Matthew 11:28

I SINCERELY BELIEVE that all Christians can live in a peace that surpasses all understanding at all times, yet it is one of the most difficult disciplines to master. I call it a discipline because it is a total surrender of our lives, dreams, fears, wants and needs at all times.

For the most part, I can get through the weeks mastering it most of the time. There are always circumstances arising to put our faith to the ultimate test.

About two weeks ago, one of the pastors in our District suddenly came down with Guillain-Barre Syndrome which is a serious disorder that occurs when the body's defense system mistakenly attacks part of the nervous system. At first he was in intensive care then was moved to a neurological ward and is now in a rehab facility. Unfortunately he cannot move his arms, or his legs. Recovery can take several weeks or even years.

It is at times like these when you lie awake at night with the thoughts fed by the enemy trying to instill doubt into your mind about an all knowing, all powerful, caring, God.

Questions arise whenever we are confronted with severe situations in our families, friends or those we care about. Around 4 one morning God woke me up with his face visible in my mind and I began to pray. While praying for him, fear gripped my heart and thoughts of doubt crept in. I pushed them away and continued to pray for him. I struggled to pray and believe God's capable Hand in Joshua's life. Only after I placed him in God's hand in a figurative way, saying to God, "You are God, the Everlasting Father, take this burden from me and may your will be done in Joshua's life", was I able to fall into a peaceful sleep again.

I woke up that morning at peace knowing that God knows the whole situation and is capable of bringing Joshua and his family through this awful situation.

Throughout my life, God has taught me severe lessons each time I doubted, worried or tried to put Him in a box. Every single thing I feared came to fruition, yet with God at my side, I went through the storm and my faith was increased and the lesson to persevere and not give in to doubt was learnt.

God's word is full of encouragement to us today that whatever the storm, we will not be left alone instead we have the peace from God to assure us that He knows about everything we are going through and His will in our lives will be accomplished.

God's grace is sufficient for every situation. I do not need the grace to survive Guillain-Barre syndrome because I do not have the sickness today. Joshua needs God's grace and will be given the strength to persevere.

There is one guarantee in life if we have a relationship with Christ He will give us what we need at the time, never before, and never after, just at the right moment.

I know that there are situations in your lives which you cannot come to peace with, but I can assure you, once you surrender it wholeheartedly to God and His will, you will have perfect rest.

I look forward to what God is going to do in Joshua and his family's life through this whole ordeal. There is nothing on this earth that we experience in vain.

It is at times like these when we pray for those who are going through illness, stressful situations and other traumas, so that we can see God's hand at work. I do believe that God hears our prayers, He stopped the oil flow in the gulf, He brought us the much needed rain this past week, He alone, will be with those in need of His miraculous touch. Of this I have no doubt.

Prayer: Lord, I am in desperate need of your grace which will strengthen and equip me for the difficult situations I face.

Your turn:

Where do you need God's Grace to pour into your situation?

[26]

Do You Hear that?

"Listen to my words, Job; pay attention to what I have to say." Job 33:1

IT IS NO SECRET that I quiver and shake in my shoes at the sight or sound of squirrels, possums, raccoons, moths, beetles, snakes, crickets or any other creature which is not human.

At 2.30 am on a Wednesday morning I woke up with my husband Stephan moving about the bedroom, banging on the ceiling, mumbling about something moving around in the ceiling. I just about had a heart attack. I do not do well at sounds in the darkness, let alone something moving around in the ceiling.

Anyone who knows me knows that I have a problem with my hearing and once I take my "ear" out (hearing aid), well, that shuts most of life out for me.

Stephan ran upstairs into the attic to see if the critter, whatever it is, made its way into the home already. He tried to coax our little tiger, (yorkie poo) Annie, to help him find the intruder, but she jumped into bed with mommy under the duvet and did not want to know about finding any creature in her home. She needed her beauty sleep, not disturbance.

After much effort trying to find and shut the intruder up, Stephan got back into bed and I asked him "What on earth is going on?" His answer to me was "Don't you hear the scratching and walking around?"

"No, how can I, I don't have my ear in." I responded grumpily

He then said "Listen, just listen." I felt panic building up instantly, my heart started racing like crazy, fear clouded my hearing. "I will never hear it" I said. He once again said "Listen, shhh, just listen."

I tried desperately not to hear anything, but the more I listened, I finally actually heard. It was as clear as if the critter was right there in the room with us. It then hit me that this is exactly how we are with God. He is trying to tell us so much about His ways and His will for our lives but we are clouded up with fear and a refusal to just be quiet and "Listen."

As the light of day came, the intruder made less noise and eventually stopped. My heart once again was at peace and everything seemed okay again. Just as the light brought quietness to the house, so listening to what God has to say to us brings us the peace that directs our path.

Prayer: God, I thank you that I can cry out to you and you hear me. Help me Lord to be able to hear you through the noise around me. Help me to listen for your voice and know when it is You speaking to me.

Your Turn:

How do you listen for God's voice? Are there times when you know He is speaking, yet, you make as if you can't "Hear" Him?

[27]

How Much is Enough

As the deer longs for streams of water, so I long for you, O God. Psalm 42:1

I have two little dogs, a Yorkie Poo named Annie and a little Chihuahua Terrier mix. They are not human beings yet their behavior is very similar.

Annie has a lot of toys which she has collected over the years. In comes Charlie, new to the family and has the nerve to want to play with her toys which she doesn't touch. She only plays with her ducky. The other toys remain new and in their bin. As Charlie finds pleasure in the toys, she decides she wants them and he has to "hand them over." Poor Charlie, he then goes to play with another toy and she proceeds to take that away from him as well. She ends up with all the toys and he sits all alone with nothing to play with.

What is the human likeness to this story? We want what others have even if we didn't want it to begin with. But when someone else has it, suddenly it is what we want.

There is a tragic account of Ahab in 1 Kings 21. Ahab saw Naboth's vineyard and decided he wanted it. When Naboth refused to give or sell it to Ahab, Ahab went home pouting to his wife, Jezebel. Jezebel devised a plan to get it which resulted in Naboth's death. Ahab got what he wanted, but the joy of it was short-lived, because Elijah showed up to spoil his gains.

How do we fight covetousness? We have to choose the right things, the right way. I'm not saying that all desire is wrong; God created us to desire and achieve. But we need to remember what is important in life.

God should be the One we long for.

" *I once thought these things were valuable, but now I consider them worthless*

because of what Christ has done."
Philippians 3:7

A man was tired of his friends owning nicer homes than his, so he went to see a realtor and put his home on the market and began to search for a new one. One day, as he was reading the paper, he came across a listing for a home that was just what he was looking for. He called his realtor. The realtor replied "Sir, that is your house. That is the house we are trying to sell for you."

God wants us to enjoy our labor and what He has blessed us with. However, life seems to get in the way and the worldview tries to convince us that we need more than we have. We need a better, bigger, home, car, or toy. None of that will bring us contentment. God will however give us our heart's desires if we focus on His ways for us.

Prayer: Please Lord help me to be content with all that I have and all that I am.

Your Turn:

What is it that you think you so desperately need that someone else has? How would your life improve if you had that item or items?

[28]

Lost in the Familiar

From the depths of despair, O Lord, I call for your help. Psalm 130:1

OUR LITTLE MALTESE Poodle Ricky is 14 ½ years old. He is blind, diabetic, has no hip joint, arthritic and has a huge lump on his neck which makes it difficult for him to swallow or chew. Yet he enjoys his little life to its fullest.

The other day I took him outside into the garden where he wanders around smelling the flowers and lifting his little leg to make sure it's his scent left behind. Usually he meanders around for a while and makes his way back to the stairs where I then pick him up and bring him inside. However, this time I saw him making his rounds in the garden and suddenly just standing in the middle of the grass with a glazed look on his face. I waited a while to see if maybe he was going to start his journey back to me, instead he continued standing there for a long while. Then I realized he was "lost" and I had to go and pick him up. When I reach him, I gently touch his little back and he jumps with excitement and waits for me to pick him up.

This reminded me of how Jesus comes to us when we have those days or moments when we feel as if we are lost and He gently touches us before He lifts us to safety. He touches us with His Spirit hoping that we will be excited at being found by Him and willingly climb into His arms for safety.

The Psalmist cries out to the Lord in the above Psalm. We often cry out to God when we feel lost or afraid.

I never want little Ricky to feel as if he is in any kind of danger or neglect, so I wait in the shadows for when I see that he needs me to help him.

This is, I believe, how God feels about us, His children. He waits in the shadows watching and if we need Him, He is there to lift us up out of despair. There will be times when you find yourself confused and maybe unsure of where to step next, even though you are in familiar surroundings. This is when you should call out to God for His strength and direction. He will hear and answer you.

Prayer: Lord you know me better than I even know myself. You have my tomorrows in your Hand and you care about everything in my life. There are many times where I feel lost even though my surroundings are familiar. These times cause me to have a lot of fear and worry in my life. Please help me Lord to rely on You more even though my life seems to be secure, help me to be secure in You.

Your Turn:

What are the times that you feel "lost" even though you are familiar with your surroundings?

Even though you may seem to have it all together, what unsettles you about your "security?"

[29]

Now What...

The Angel replied, " The Holy Spirit will come upon you, and the power of the Most High will overshadow you." Luke 1:35

CHRISTMAS IS OVER. We have had our fill of busy days, enough chocolates to feed an army, and the dessert, way too much but we could not forgo because our favorite family members either baked it or brought it.

Now that the celebration of the birth of Christ is over, what do we do with Jesus? Thankfully, God's Word is packed with instruction for our lives with Him.

You and I have placed our faith in Jesus Christ and have invited Him to come live within us, the Holy Spirit comes upon us, and the most amazing transformation happens. We have the power of God overshadowing us. We do not conceive a physical life, but the spiritual life of Jesus in the Person of the Holy Spirit.

The indwelling powerful Person of the Holy Spirit sets us free from the habits of sin. The power we possess to live a life pleasing to God is directly related to how much control of my life I give to the Holy Spirit. He convicts us and guides our actions, but we still say yes or no to His direction and conviction.

Thankfully, Jesus came many years ago, we do not have to go through the waiting process of what happened at Calvary, we have His Spirit in us, everything is possible with God. Now, we get to walk out being the Light of Christ, sharing His Hope which is Salvation, being a Christian is that wonderful life.

Yesterday and all it held is gone forever, today once again we begin the week rushing off to work and our lives go on. Hopefully this year your focus will be different. Because of who you are in Christ. Continue to move forward in your relationship with Him. Our lives change, we transform into becoming more Christ-like. The decisions we make are different from a year ago and our attitudes are different because of the fresh memory of Christ's birth in our minds.

Let every day be fresh with God. Invite Him into your day and ask Him for guidance, direction and peace. He came so that we can experience all He has to give. This is powerful. Don't ever accept lies about who you are in Christ. You are a new creation with a purpose uniquely designed for you.

Prayer: Thank you God for sending your Son Jesus so that I can have a life of fulfillment. Help me to realize who I am in Christ. Help me to see myself as that new creation with a purpose designed by you.

Your turn:

Do you walk as that person who is a New Creation in Christ? Or do you still walk your life as "the Old Man?"

What is your mindset today?

[30]

God breathes Life into Man.

Then the Lord God formed the man from the dust of the ground. He breathed the breath of life into the man's nostrils, and the man became a living person.
Genesis 2:7

TAKE A DEEP BREATH for a moment and think of the phenomenal beginning of "man." Whenever I fall into the world's thinking system of success and what others think I should be or do, I feel as if a weight is on my shoulders. My mind clouds out the promises and truths of God's Word and who He is and His plan for my life.

God had everything good in mind for "man" but as we know the rest of the account of Creation, God created woman to be a helpmate for the man and to keep him company. Unfortunately sin crept in and

99

destroyed what God intended for good, or so the enemy of our souls thought.

God had a plan of redemption to restore mankind to Himself so that He could accomplish all He has for Him.

Today we do not have evil slithering around, instead we have the world and all its pressures trying to fit us into a mold that God had not designed for us.

What is the world doing to you and which design are you trying to squeeze into, yet are so uncomfortable trying to "fit" into?

The design for your life is so wonderful; you will experience a divine un-natural peace in your heart, despite the circumstances you find yourself in. You will be adjusting to the design which God made uniquely for you and you are ignoring the dark, depressing, peace stealing mold, the slithering world wants you to be in.

The enemy of your soul wants you to continue to live in the world's system. He does not want you to accept God's plan for your life and live in peace and bearing fruit for God. He literally hates everything created by God, yet lies and deceives us into living a substandard lifestyle.

Today I want to encourage you to walk tall, accepting God's unique mold for your life. If you are not experiencing that peace which I am speaking about, then take some time out of your busy schedule, go to a quiet place and speak to your Creator who is able to once again breathe life into your nostrils, and that life is one of fulfillment.

God breathes life into us, Satan wants to suffocate us. Which life would you rather live as? A man or woman being suffocated by the lies and lifestyle of the world? Or as one accepting the breath of God breathed into you so that you can bear fruit and live in an attitude of peace.

Prayer: Thank you Jesus for coming and dying for me on the cross so that I can live in an attitude of peace, despite my circumstances. Help me to accept that You have created me unique.

Your Turn:

How are you living your life today? As a person believing the truth from God about who you are? Or. As a person believing the lies of Satan who suffocates you?

[31]

The Tide will Turn

Yet I am confident I will see the Lord's goodness while I am here in the land of the living. Wait patiently for the LORD; be brave and courageous. Yes, wait patiently for the Lord. Psalm 27:13-14

HARRIET BEECHER STOWE ONCE noted: "When you get in a tight place and everything goes against you, till it seems you could not hold on a minute longer, never give up then, for that is just the place and time that the tide will turn.

There are so many times we read in the bible about when the tide turned in just the right time. Haman conspired to kill all the Jews in the kingdom of Persia and was building a gallows on which to execute Queen Esther's uncle and she begged the king to spare her people.

Baby Moses was being set afloat in a basket in the reeds of the Nile River, God was compelling Pharaoh's daughter to go down to the river to bathe in precisely the place where she would hear the baby's cries.

God ordered Joshua to carry the ark of the Lord into the waters. As they did, the waters of the Jordan dried immediately so that all the Israelites could pass over on dry land.

Jesus calmed the sea with the command, "Peace, be Still."

The Lord honors our trust in Him to deliver us from all evil. We are commanded to trust Him without reservation or hesitation and to leave the outcome up to Him. He is the only one we can rely on to show us what to do, when to act and how to respond when it seems time is running out. Our trust in Him is a sign of resolve to be strong in Him.

Trust in the LORD with all your heart; do not depend on your own understanding. Seek His will in all you do, and He will show you which path to take. Proverbs 3:5-6

I want to encourage you today that whatever it is you may be going through, give it to the one who wants to help you carry your heavy load.

Prayer: Help me Jesus to wait until You change my circumstances. Give me the strength to hang in or to quit if that is Your will for the situation. Show me Lord what You want me to do.

Your Turn:

What are you currently facing where you feel like you cannot hang in there anymore? A job? A relationship? Ask God to show you what He wants you to do.

[32]

Fear, the 4 legged Monster

For God has not given us a spirit of fear and timidity, but of power, love and self-discipline. 2 Timothy 1:7

EVER HEAR statements such as "if you do not eat all your food on your plate, God will punish you."

"If you do not... God will punish you"

"You are not well because you have sinned against God and He is punishing you..."

Threats of God's punishment flow freely from some people's lips. Even before they have thought the sentence of judgment through once, they create fear.

Growing up in the late 50's and throughout my life, God has been used to cause fear in me even though I was trying my best to serve Him in my everyday life. Fear was put into me either by parents, teachers, or leaders who were trying to manipulate us to either behave or do our chores. It was not necessarily their fault that was how it was way back when.

We read in 1 John 5:3 ...***And his commands are not burdensome,*** for everyone born of God overcomes the world. This is the victory that has overcome the world, even our faith.

Who overcomes the world? Us who believe that Jesus is the Son of God.

Strange how even though this Scripture was read back then, only the fact that we were to fear God was emphasized. I can never remember Scriptures such as this one in 1 John in a positive way because it was drowned out by those Scriptures drummed into me about God's judgment on us. I struggled to overcome the world because I never really knew that I *was in Christ.* All I could concentrate on was the reality that God was going to condemn me.

I am not saying that we must not respect God with a righteous fear because that is the beginning of knowledge (Proverbs 1:7) But having so much fear in our lives can and does actually prevent us from realizing who we are in Christ and walking with confidence overcoming the world and its lies. God continually gives of Himself to all of us, it is this beautiful gift that we must hang on to and pass on to those who are in the world without a Hope, because they are the ones who should walk in fear of God.

My challenge to you today is. Are you walking around in fear? Fearing what the day will bring, fearing that God will not show you favor? It is time to accept that Christ has overcome the world, we are confident of this. We have Him living within us and He is willing to take us through every single trial and circumstance giving us a sense of joy and peace. He also wants us to pass on to others this Hope that we have in Him.

Join me today in letting go of those things that we fear and trusting God who loves us to show us His way.

Prayer: Lord thank you for the truth and it is your truth that sets me free. I am an overcomer Lord because of who I am in You. Help me Lord to walk in the way You have designed for me. Help me to let go of the fear I have in my heart. Fear that I will never be able to please

you. Fear that you will condemn me if I make mistakes.

Your Turn:

What do you fear?

[33]

Goodbye Old Man

We know that our old sinful selves were crucified with Christ so that sin might lose its power in our lives. We are no longer slaves to sin. Romans 6:6

THERE HAVE BEEN TIMES when I felt like running away. Not for any reason other than from myself. Ever felt like that? Then reality sinks in and I am able to focus on the fact that I can never ever run away from myself. If situations seem awful, I am there, my thinking and rationalizing about the situation is the same if I am in my home in East Rockaway or if I am in Timbuktu. I am there, with all my habits, and history engrained in my heart, mind and blood.

My reactions are so well rehearsed and engrained, that before I can think about how or what I must do, I have judged, and decided how I need to act. What I perceive the situation to be is not always the truth.

God's Word gives us the answer to this problem.

When we accept Christ as our Personal Savior and Ruler of our lives, He begins His work of change deep within. Daily we need to set our mind on things above, not on things on the earth for we died, and our lives are hidden with Christ in God. We put to death our evil desires and covetousness, as well as anger, wrath, malice, blasphemy, filthy language and we put on the new man who is renewed in knowledge according to the image of Him who created us. (Colossians 3:2-10)

Every time I witness believers going through the waters of baptism, it reminds me of the real person I am.Those well-rehearsed and engrained reactions can and will change as I submit myself wholly to Christ and His Spirit who lives in me bringing about those changes needed so that I can become the person God created me to be. This is such an awesome feeling of peace which comes over me when I surrender everything to God. I surrender my dreams, my failures, my successes, my hopes and my plans. Then He can work in me.

Goodbye old man, hello new man who is renewed in knowledge according to the image of Him who created me.

Today, accept the fact that if you have accepted Christ as your Savior, you are no longer the old man, instead you are the new man renewed in knowledge according to the image of Him who created you.

Prayer: Jesus, thank you that I am no longer the person who was consumed with the things of this world. Thank you that I am that new man, renewed in knowledge according to your image. You created me and I thank you for making me wonderfully unique.

Your Turn:

What parts of your old nature are you still trying to put behind you?

What parts of your new nature have you allowed God to clothe you with?

[34]

Fear-Filled Future

So don't worry in advance about how to answer the charges against you, for I will give you the right words and such wisdom that none of your opponents will be able to reply or refute you! Luke 21:14-15

THESE VERSES DESCRIBE how we are to react during fear filled times. Us, as Jesus' disciples should respond in a fearless manner. We trust our Master wholeheartedly. When life seems to spin out of control, Jesus asks us not to worry because we will have the words and wisdom when our adversaries seem to be so eloquent and irrefutable.

We are warned here in this portion that we will be betrayed by the very people we love. Jesus was not promising a physical shield of protection that will drop down to surround us, but He is speaking spiritually

– even if we are put to death we will not be harmed spiritually.

We are all faced with times of fear. Even watching the news can upset your stomach. Again Jesus says we are not to fear. The feelings of fear that grip our hearts have to be arrested and we must replace these feelings with confidence in God. Whenever we are betrayed, either by those we love or by others, God says that we must stand firm in our faith and He will fight the battle for us.

Remember, the battle belongs to the Lord.

The first portion of this scripture tells us that before we go through the betrayal period we must make up our minds how we will defend ourselves and that we will not worry. How will we prepare ourselves? By reading God's Word every day, spending time with Him so that we are secure in our relationship with Him. We will KNOW our God and in Him we will trust.

There are many things that cause fear in our hearts. The financial situation in the world seems to be so rocky. Jobs are not stable. Our healthcare is in trouble and the fear of terrorism lurks around every corner. We do not know who will be our next president and there are times that we are concerned about this. We do not know what crisis is around the corner, but what we do know is that God will always be with us and see us through any political, financial, relational or other turmoil or change. So always remember, God is in control therefore we do not fear.

Prayer: Help me Jesus to remember that you have my tomorrows in your hand. Help me to place everything that I fear at your feet. Give me your peace which surpasses all understanding and equip me for any situation or circumstance I am going to face.

Your turn:

Write down your fears that you want God to take away from you. Release them to His care and wait for His peace to cover you.

[35]

GOD'S WHISPER

...And after the fire there was the sound of a gentle whisper. 1 Kings 19:12

Have you ever TRIED TO "HEAR FROM GOD" AND THEN STARTED TO LOOK FOR His answer in your circumstances or surroundings? When Hurricane Sandy hit us, I tried desperately to hear what God was saying to us in the storm. During the noise of the storm I feverishly looked for my answer, yet never got it.

After the wind calmed down, the rain eased up and the water started to recede back to its limits, that's when I sensed God's whisper in my heart.

Immediately neighbors reached out to one another, making sure that needs were met. Relief Centers were opened and people were networking between one another trying to be the hands and feet God wanted them to be. This was when I saw God at work in a massive approach.

As awful as the disaster was, I clearly saw God's healing hand throughout. Neighbors spoke to one another and reached out to help like never before. Usually, everyone is unaware of what is going on in another person's life, yet this was an opportunity for us to get into many people's lives, bringing words of encouragement where we were never able to before.

During the storm, the experience had by people was not gentle at all. Many lost their entire contents of their homes. It was after the storm that God's hand was quietly moving through the overwhelmed Island.

It is during times of stress and confusion that we try to hear God speak to us. The noise of calamity, whether from a storm or negative situation in our lives, does not lend itself to God's voice being heard. Whenever we quieten our hearts and focus our entire being on God, waiting for Him to give us the much needed peace over our minds, hearts and souls, then He manages to get through to us.

My word of encouragement to you today is that you separate yourself from the noise of your "storm" (circumstance.) Go to God where in the quiet of your heart, He can whisper your name.

Prayer: Jesus, thank you that even though my circumstances are causing a lot of stress in me, I can come to you, quieten my heart before You and You will whisper my name and talk to me.

Your Turn:

What is the situation right now that you are facing wherein you cannot seem to "hear" God?

[36]

Mirror Mirror, on the wall

"For if you listen to the word and don't obey, it is like glancing at your face in a mirror. You see yourself, walk away and forget what you look like." James 1:23-24

DAY IN AND DAY OUT, we get opportunities to look at ourselves in a mirror. Sometimes we see that we need to brush our hair, or wipe dirt off our faces. Rarely do we walk away from the mirror forgetting what we have just seen or experienced. By experience I mean sometimes we are not too pleased with the new wrinkle we discovered or the sagging chin.

If we see our hair is a mess, we do something about it, dirt on our face? It gets wiped off. The sagging chin or wrinkle however is not something we can do to reverse it. We might try to prevent further sagging or wrinkling.

Each day begins with our time with God. We read Scripture and lay our petitions at His feet, and then off to work we go. Life gets stressful and situations cause the peace we began our day with to disappear.

A great example is: If our devotions took us to Psalm 46 which says: God is our refuge and strength, an ever-present help in trouble. Therefore we will not fear, though the earth gives way and the mountains fall into the heart of the sea, though its waters roar and foam and the mountains quake with their surging.

After reading this Psalm we will get up from our time with God feeling protected and safe. However, this may not last very long. In other words, we have just forgotten what we read.

God brings to mind the Scripture just as we will look in the mirror and "see" ourselves clearly, so too, we must get up from our time with God and face the day with confidence not forgetting what we read and claiming back the peace that we had when we spent our time with God.

This takes practice, but it is possible. I certainly do not forget the new wrinkles found when looking in the mirror, or the sagging eyes, so I know that it is possible to walk in the same way I felt when spending time with God. I just need to practice it more.

Daily, as you look in the mirror, remember you can walk in God's words to you each day and be strengthened.

Prayer: Jesus please help me to re-member what you have whispered to me from Your Word. Help me not to forget what I have just experienced during my time with you.

Your turn:

Do you ever forget what God has told you after you have read His Word?

Have you ever forgotten what you look like in the mirror?

[37]

Jesus wants to calm the Storm in your life today

When Jesus woke up, He rebuked the wind and said to the waves, "Silence! Be still!" Suddenly the wind stopped, and there was a great calm. Mark 4:39

I KNOW FOR A FACT that if Jesus was in the boat of your life today, He would say to you, "Why are you so afraid? Do you still have no faith?" Take a few moments and look at the situation of your life today. What are you worried about? The future, the world arena, fears of terrorism, inflation, your children's education, who will they marry, what will they do for a living? How are you going to pay all the bills when everything just keeps getting more and more expensive and your income is not going up with inflation?

God wants to discuss everything with you. Everything that is of a concern to you, as well as what is a blessing to you. He wants you to recognize the blessings given to you by Him on a daily basis. Do you spend time with God, reading His Word praying and then when you get up from your time with Him, it's back to normal? Worry, worry, stress and anger? In Verse 38 the disciples woke Jesus and said to him, *"**Teacher, don't you care that we're going to drown?**"* I'm sure today you say the same thing to God, "God, don't you care if...?"

The disciples realized that Jesus was someone who was different. The waves and the wind obeyed Him. Now that same Jesus, can calm the storm in your life. I'm not saying that the consequences of actions will be miraculously taken away, but he most certainly will be with you and give you the calm you need. He will help you not to make any more of the wrong decisions.

If you are still striving to "fix" your own problems and circumstances, you will just go around in circles until you learn to place it at the feet of Jesus and leave it there. Scripture says, we have enough to worry about for today, tomorrow will bring its own cares.

Ask God to undertake in your situation, and do not doubt when you are asking, and remember nothing is too difficult for Him, nor too small. If you pray, yet in your mind you doubt saying, "Yeah right..." Don't even bother praying, because if you doubt, you will never get what you are praying for. On the other hand however, you will get whatever you ask for if you have "FAITH" in God who is the only one who can help you.

There are some people who have become comfortable with the feelings of stress and misery, that they really don't want God to help them, and then they won't get His help.

Trust God completely with your entire life and be anxious for nothing and present all your needs to him prayer with thanksgiving and see the Lord direct your life and work out his perfect plan for you.

Prayer: Help me God to remember to bring everything to you in prayer, thanking you and believing that my situation is taken care of because of You. There may be rough tides ahead of me, but with You I know that I can get through any situation.

Your Turn:

What situation do you want God to undertake for you right now?

What are you trusting God with in your life?

[38]

I finally Get It!

Dear children, don't let anyone deceive you about this: When people do what is right, it shows that they are righteous, even as Christ is righteous.
1 John 3:7

ONE OF THE MOST frustrating things we deal with as Christians is the reality that not everyone sees Christ as we do. We experience this amazing relationship with the Creator of the Universe. Each day we can come into His presence without hesitation, knowing that He hears every word we say to Him. He smiles on us, He loves on us and we walk in a peace that we wish everyone could experience.

I often suggest that the emotion of fear should *not* be active and life changing. It should be a word with no power whatsoever. Faith on the other hand, well now, that is a verb. It should be a life transforming word. By faith each day we come into God's presence, thanking Him in advance for all He does and for how He is going to answer our prayers.

How can we so boldly do this?

Ever had an "aha" moment? This is one of those. Those of us who have accepted Christ as our personal Savior are children of God. We walk each day guided by His Spirit, not listening to the lies of the enemy trying to deceive us that we should be fearful of the future, fearful of tomorrow, nor even fearful of today.

Ever thought about reaching for that cup of coffee? No! you just reach for it. Ever thought about how you just know to brush your teeth? No! you just brush your teeth. This is the same thing with the verb, Faith! You literally do the Christ walk. Asking God each day to work through you helping someone who does not have the Hope you do, to accept that Christ is their Hope and life.

John goes on to say that we who are from God have overcome the world because of the reality of Christ being in us and He is greater than those in the world. (1 John 4:4)

I am so excited about walking by faith each day because each day is full of promise and not compromise. Each day God guides me forward and I try not to look back at my failures, but towards the Hope of Him working through me transforming lives of those whom He places in my path. It is so amazing to see His Hand working and lives changing. He is still God and on the Throne.

My challenge to you today is: Get Up! Accept the challenge of Christ in You. He is greater than the little word fear. He is the action word Faith. Amazing things begin to happen when you move knowing He is your guide.

Prayer: Jesus I am so excited that I can get up and face today with a confidence so strong because I have You guiding and going before me. You are still God and on the Throne. Help me to accept the challenges that are before me today.

Your Turn:

What prevents you from walking into your day with that confidence which only comes by knowing that God is with You?

[39]

Wounds that won't Heal

Everyday circumstances reveal God's Hand in our lives and surroundings. My little dog was licking his leg constantly and as much as I rebuked him, he would not listen to me. He just kept licking. Soon the little wound on his leg became severely infected, swollen and painful. He kept licking, trying to heal his little wound, instead it became worse.

When I was fighting with him to stop trying to fix his wound, God impressed on my heart how we as human beings are constantly doing that. We try to heal our own wounds instead of allowing Him access to it so that He can bring about a healing that will last.

Eventually little Ricky had no option but to let us clean his wound, cut the hair around it, put on Neosporin and finally close it with a plaster. Three days later, his wound was healing quickly and we still nursed it until it was completely healed.

What God wants us to do is come to Him with our open wounds, giving Him full access to pour on His healing balm, allow Him to do whatever He needs to do so that our wounds will heal completely. There may be scars left behind but they are reminders to us of God's healing hand on our lives. Those scars testify to the awesome faithfulness of a God who is interested in us to the point of wanting to be involved in healing our wounds.

If you have open wounds today, allow God full access to the raw pain so that permanent healing can take place. He is our healer not only of physical diseases but also of wounds that won't heal without His help.

God reveals Himself to us all the time. His creation speaks of His wonders and awesome power. Each morning as the sun rises His hand is seen clearly by the magnificence of its bright and powerful life giving source. Seasons change and His craftsmanship is spread all over the world for us to enjoy and be encouraged that we serve an awesome God who by the mere mention of words He spoke everything into existence.

He uniquely and lovingly created mankind to worship Him and to enjoy His creation. Allow Him this morning to apply His healing balm and gently bring about complete healing to those inner wounds.

Prayer: Lord Jesus, you know the wounds I have and how painful they are. You know that they keep me from completely living that life of fulfillment You want me to live. Heal me Lord completely. Touch me and help me to move on, regardless of my scars.

Your Turn:

What wounds do you have and want to bring to Christ to heal today?

[40]

In the Middle of Danger, Yet, secure!

For I hold you by your right hand – I, the Lord your God. And I say to you, "Don't be afraid. I am here to help you." Isaiah 41:13

IT WAS IN MARCH of 2012 that we realized there were "mice" in our home. These little furry critters were not welcome at all. Traps were set with cheese as bait, but to our disgust we saw that they managed somehow to eat the cheese out and yet not set the trap "off."

We never realized just how bad the whole situation was and thought that maybe it was one or two little mice coming in from out of the cold to find some warmth and food.

My husband, Stephan went off to South Africa and I was left to "man the fort" alone. I have always been of the mindset that nothing will make me not accomplish what I need to do because of fear so I ignored seeing the dog trying to dig under the kitchen cupboard because she heard something moving inside. You know the response well, ignore something and it might go away? Not likely.

It was on a Friday morning and I was speaking to Steve on the phone. It was very early and I was still in bed. From the corner of my eye I saw something move and I sat up in absolute shock at what I saw. Here was this little mouse, running around the bedroom floor, looking for food and not even flinching at me screaming and squeaking. I said to Steve "There is a mouse in the bedroom, do something." He responded "What on earth must I do from South Africa, go and get some traps and set them all over the house, just in case." I yelled back "no way, you get home now, I'm booking you a flight home, and I'm moving out until you get here to take care of the mice."

I then decided I was going to move out of the house into Steve's office until he got home. I knew that this was silly, but my initial reaction was "fear"

I did not move out of course, as I pulled myself together but I did move out of the bedroom and the dogs and I made our little room in the living room where we thought we would be mouse free, because after all, they were seen in the bedroom, never in the living room. I closed the kitchen off and sealed the doors, as I knew they moved around the kitchen during the night.

The whole point of telling you this story is this. When Steve got home three days later, we set fresh traps and caught 17 mice in total. The funniest thing about the whole issue was that even though there was a little mouse seen in the bedroom, there were 16 other mice running around where I was sleeping at night. But, I did not know that.

The lesson I learned from this whole infestation was that even though I was in the middle of all these creatures, I felt safe. I never saw them so I never realized the real situation. It made me grasp God's awesome amount of protection covering all of us even though we do not know the danger lurking maybe a few inches away from us. We feel safe because we do not see the danger.

Through this whole experience, I believe that God wants to encourage us with the realization that He sees the whole situation for what it is and knows that we do not need to see the danger around us because we will not handle it well.

Whatever situation you find yourself in, remember that we must rest in a God who sees everything, He knows the dangers lurking around us, yet He wants us to trust Him. He gives us what we can handle, He lets us see what we can cope with.

Remember when the Israelites left Egypt, God told Moses not to go on the road through the Philistine country, though that was shorter. The account of the Exodus is like this. **When Pharoah finally let the people go, God did not lead them along the main road that runs through Philistine territory, even though that was the shortest route to the Promised Land. God said, "If the people are faced with a battle, they might change their minds and return to Egypt Exodus 13:17-18.**

We need not fear anything, God sees it before we do and He directs our path safely and lovingly. There are times when He leads us down a longer path to get to our destination, but it's because He knows what we can handle and He sees the danger.

Prayer: Jesus, help me to rest in You, Lord. Help me to place my complete trust in You. You see the whole picture. You know where the dangers lurk and You know what I can handle.

Your Turn:

What is the situation you find yourself in that you must trust God with completely?